Pebble® Plus

Animal Offspring

# Dogs and Their Puppies

Revised Edition

Linda Tagliaferro

raintree

a Capstone company — publishers for children

Raintree is an imprint of Capstone Global Library Limited, a company incorporated in England and Wales having its registered office at 264 Banbury Road, Oxford, OX2 7DY – Registered company number: 6695582

www.raintree.co.uk
myorders@raintree.co.uk

ISBN 978 1 4747 5626 6
22 21 20 19 18
10 9 8 7 6 5 4 3 2 1

**British Library Cataloging in Publication Data**
A full catalogue record for this book is available from the British Library.

**Editorial Credits**
Gina Kammer, editor; Sarah Bennett, designer; Morgan Walters, media researcher; Katy LaVigne, production specialist

Printed and bound in India.

**Acknowledgements**
We would like to thank the following for permission to reproduce photographs:
Shutterstock: Anna Goroshnikova, right 21, Anna Hoychuk, 15, Burry van den Brink, 19, Christian Mueller, Cover, Fernando Castelani, right 20, left 21, framsook, 5, Grigorita Ko, 1, 17, Kristin Castenschiold, 7, Nadya Chetah, 9, Nixx Photography, left 20, Sarune Kairyte, 11, Stephen Coburn, 13

# Contents

# Dogs

Dogs are mammals.
Young dogs are
called puppies.

Male and female dogs mate.

Female dogs give birth

to a litter of puppies.

# Puppies

Puppies cannot see
or hear until they are
about ten days old.

Puppies sleep most of
the time. Puppies get tired
from playing.

Puppies drink milk

from their mother

for about five weeks.

# Growing up

Puppies can eat dog food
when they are about
six weeks old.

Puppies jump on and play with each other. They chew toys.

Puppies become adults
after one to two years.

# Watch dogs grow

birth

20

adult after
about two years

# Glossary

**adult** animal that is able to mate

**litter** group of puppies born at the same time to the same mother; dogs usually have litters of four to six puppies

**mammal** warm-blooded animal that has a backbone; most mammals have hair or fur; female mammals feed milk to their young

**mate** join together to produce young

# Find out more

## Books

*A Dog's Day*, Rebecca Rissman (Raintree, 2014)

*A Dog's Life* (Watch It Grow), Louise Spilsbury (Raintree, 2011)

*Dogs and Puppies* (Animals and Their Babies), Annabelle Lynch (Franklin Watts, 2016)

## Websites

www.animalark.co.uk/indexbafc.html?PageId=dogs
Animal Ark

www.bbc.co.uk/cbeebies/puzzles/puppy-quiz
BBC

# Comprehension questions

1. What are puppies like just after they are born?

2. What is the word used for a group of puppies born at the same time?

3. How do puppies change as they grow into dogs?

# Index